BEYOND

BROKE

A Guide To Unlocking 10 Core Keys To

Wealth And Security

Brad M. Fenderson

Copyright

Table Of Content

Contents

Introduction

Accomplishing and maintaining a stable monetary position is really important for many individuals and families. It lays the foundation for a no-problem future and can help you achieve your financial goals. You can work on your monetary soundness and security by complying with the 10 Core Keys to Wealth and Security, which are a bunch of rules that can direct you in the correct direction.

Making a spending plan is the most vital move towards achieving and keeping up with monetary steadiness. An arrangement for how you will spend and set aside your cash is known as a financial plan. It ought to detail all of your pay as well as your uses, and it ought to be refreshed consistently. A spending plan is a valuable device that can help you keep up with your monetary objectives and guarantee that your spending is in accordance with your pay.

The next significant step is to save cash for your retirement. To arrive at a state where one is secure financially, saving cash for the future is fundamental. It can help you with assembling a backup stash, setting aside cash for retirement, and preparing for unexpected expenses. It is fundamental to put away cash on a predictable premise and to brilliantly contribute.

The next significant step is to dispose of obligations. The weight of obligations can be a huge obstruction to achieving long-term monetary security. It is basic to get free from existing obligations as fast as could be expected and to avoid assuming any extra obligations.

The formation of a rainy-day account is the fourth significant stage. An investment account assigned for use in case of unanticipated expenses is alluded to as a secret stash. It is critical to have a secret stash in the event that you lose your employment, need to pay for clinical consumption, or whatever else emerges out of the blue.

The next significant variable is to make sharp ventures. Placing cash on the securities exchange is one of the best ways to accumulate wealth and secure one's monetary future. It is fundamental to investigate the numerous potential open doors for effective financial planning and to have a comprehension of the perils that are associated with every decision.

Shielding oneself from deceitful monetary action is the next significant stage. It is vital to avoid the potential risk of monetary extortion, as the commonality of the issue keeps on rising. This includes keeping an eye on your credit record, picking passwords that are challenging to figure out, and monitoring normal cheats.

The next recommendation is to foster sound examples of conduct about cash. If you have any desire to be financially capable, you ought to attempt to live within your means, abstain from making rash purchases, and pay your instalments on time.

Getting instruction is another basic step. Acquiring monetary security requires getting training in monetary issues. It is fundamental to not just have a principal comprehension of individual budgets but additionally to be current on any pertinent new turns of events.

Having a methodology for when you resign is also another fundamental stage. Making arrangements for one's retirement years is a fundamental part of acquiring long-term monetary security. It is fundamental to have a comprehension of the numerous potential outcomes accessible for retirement as well as to get ready for what's in store.

Counselling a specialist is the next piece of prompt I can give you. With regards to laying out monetary security, the help of an expert guide might be of gigantic use. It is vital to look for the direction of a proficient expert, whether it be a monetary guide or one more sort of master.

It is workable for you to acquire monetary strength and security by following these 10 keys to Wealth and Security. On the off chance that you keep these rules, you will actually want to lay out a stable monetary future for yourself and understand your monetary goals.

Chapter 1

The Meaning Of Monetary Steadiness

A state of one's monetary wellbeing and prosperity is intended to be conveyed by the expression "monetary steadiness." It is an estimation of a person's or, alternately, an association's ability to satisfy its monetary responsibilities, like taking care of bills, making instalments on time, and keeping a decent FICO rating. This might be a positive or negative term. Dependability in one's monetary circumstances is basic for individuals and organisations, as well as for states.

Security in one's monetary circumstance might be accomplished when an individual or association has adequate assets to take care of their commitments as a whole and living expenses, as well as having the option to set aside cash to the side for their future needs. It is an estimation of an individual or association's monetary security and strength, and deciding the degree of hazard that they pose is frequently utilized. Strength in one's individual accounting records is fundamental for individuals since it empowers them to keep a solid FICO rating, which, thus, may simplify it for them to get credits, visas, and numerous other types of customer support.

Furthermore, it is fundamental for organisations to keep up with their monetary stability. It makes it simpler for organisations to have a solid income, which is fundamental for both their tasks and their development. It helps organisations in actually dealing with their dangers and guaranteeing that they have the assets to pay their instalments and different commitments.

The support of a stable monetary position is one more need for legislatures. To meet their commitments to their kin and pay off their obligations, states have a commitment to ensure that they have adequate monetary assets available to them. It is likewise essential for states to save monetary solidity to keep their economies sound and to ensure that their populace approaches a full scope of monetary labour and products.

Various powers cooperate to create stable monetary circumstances. These include having a fair FICO rating, adequate assets to meet one's bills as well as one's commitments, and a strong investment fund system. Moreover, it is fundamental to have a strong cognizance of the different monetary labour and products accessible and to know about the dangers that are associated with utilising them.

Getting and keeping up with monetary steadiness ought to be really important for all gatherings included, including individuals, organisations, and legislatures. It is an estimation of both monetary security and monetary strength, and it is fundamental for supporting areas of strength and giving admission to different monetary labour and products. It is fundamental to have a strong comprehension of the components that add to one's monetary dependability and to make dynamic moves to guarantee that one is in a position where they are not in danger of losing their monetary balance.

Chapter 2

Key 1: Laying Out A Financial Plan

Making a spending plan is quite possibly one of the most vital undertakings that should be undertaken to arrive at a condition of monetary solidity. An arrangement that outlines how you need to spend and set aside your cash is referred to as a financial plan. It is useful in guaranteeing that your enjoyment is as per the money-related targets that you have set for yourself. You will actually want to watch your spending, decide your monetary needs, and verify that you are not overspending by setting up a financial plan.

The principal thing you want to do to make a financial plan is to monitor the entirety of your income and spending. Give a rundown of every one of the methods by which you can get cash, including your ordinary pay, any ventures you might have, and any extra techniques. From that point onward, make a rundown of the entirety of your expenses, including your lease, your utilities, your food, and some other bills. You can begin dealing with a financial plan after you have gathered a rundown of the entirety of your income and spending.

The next thing you really want to do is lay out a few financial targets. What are a portion of your more immediate as well as broader monetary goals? Would you like to take care of cash for another home, a vehicle, or your brilliant years? Do you wish to get free from your obligations? Laying out targets can help you keep up with the centre of your monetary arrangement and guarantee that you utilise the cash you have accessible to you.

In the wake of concluding how you need to manage your cash, you can begin dealing with a financial plan. To get everything rolling, make separate spending plans for each of your various kinds of consumption. You may, for example, make a spending plan for the lease, the power, the food, and whatever other costs you have. You ought to likewise make a different financial plan for your speculations and investment funds. Be certain that the targets you are laying out are feasible and that you can remain focused on them.

To wrap things up, you ought to regularly analyse your monetary arrangement. Ensure that you are not going amiss with your spending plan and that it is as per the goals that you have set for your funds. Changes should be made to your spending plan if you find that you are going over your spending limit in certain classes.

Fostering a spending plan and adhering to it is an essential move towards achieving monetary security. It helps you monitor your spending, lay out monetary targets for yourself, and guarantee that you are not spending more than you acquire. You will actually want to build a spending plan that will help you arrive at your financial targets, assuming that you follow these stages all together.

Advantages Of Planning

The production of a spending plan is a fundamental chapter of having a secure monetary balance. It guarantees that people and families have their funds all together while additionally helping them make arrangements for what's to come. Making a financial plan permits one to monitor their spending, moderate cash, and guarantee that their instalments are paid on time. Also, it might help with bringing down obligations and expanding investment funds.

The capacity of people and families to all the more likely get ready for what's in store is the essential benefit that comes from utilising a financial plan. People can lay out monetary targets for them and measure their advancement towards achieving those objectives when they make a spending plan. This may help in guaranteeing that individuals are taking care of adequate assets for retirement, training, or other long-term goals. Notwithstanding this advantage, planning might help individuals and families get ready for unforeseen expenses, for example, those related to hospital expenses or vehicle upkeep.

A second benefit of planning is that it helps people and families monitor the cash that they spend. People might figure out where their cash is going to go to guarantee that they are not overspending by fostering a spending plan to direct their monetary choices. This may help people as well as families by avoiding obligations and setting aside cash for what's in store. What's more, planning might help people and families decide regions in which they can reduce their consumption and increase how much cash they save.

The third benefit of creating and adhering to a financial plan is that it makes it simpler for people and families to pay their costs on time. People who set up a financial plan for themselves are better prepared to get ready for approaching instalments and guarantee that they are paid on time. This might help with staying away from late expenses as well as different sorts of punishments. Likewise, planning might help people and families recognise regions in which they can limit their costs, for example, by changing to a telephone plan with lower month-to-month expenses or bringing down how much energy they use.

At long last, making a spending plan might help people and families take care of their obligations and develop their reserve funds over the long run. People who make a spending plan are better prepared to distinguish regions in which they might bring down their obligations, for example, taking care of visas or school credits, and can do whatever it may take to do so. Also, planning might help individuals and families perceive regions in which they can possibly improve their investment funds, for example, by expanding how much cash they set aside for their retirement or a secret stash.

Making a spending plan is a fundamental chapter of achieving and keeping up with monetary security. People and families might profit from its capacity to assist them with making arrangements for the future, monitor their spending, guarantee that their bills are paid on time, limit their obligations, and raise their investment funds. Creating and adhering to a spending plan is one of the most mind-blowing ways of promising one's monetary security and steadiness.

Instructions To Make A Financial Plan

1. Decide on your drawn-out monetary targets: Before you can make a spending plan, you should initially figure out how you need to manage your cash. Invest some energy in reflecting on what it is that you need to accomplish, both in the short term and further away.

2. Watch your spending. If you have any desire to have the option to develop a financial plan for yourself, you really want to know where your cash is going. If you have any desire to get a better picture of where your cash is going and the amount you're spending, monitor your consumption for a month.

3. Decide your pay: Decide your absolute month-to-month pay by including each of your types of revenue, for example, your

compensation, any ventures you have, and some other cash you get.

4. Register your month-to-month uses: Figure your general month-to-month expenses, which ought to incorporate leases, utilities, food, and whatever other costs you have.

5. Make a financial plan. Make a financial plan for each sort of expenditure you mean to make. Ensure you leave some room in your financial plan for unforeseen expenses.

6. Lay out a reserve fund plan. Laying out a reserve fund plan will help you accomplish your financial goals. Ponder moving cash from your financial records to your bank account consistently, utilising a mechanised exchange.

7. Watch your advancement: Monitor how far along you are in accomplishing your financial goals. This will help you keep up with your inspiration and stay focused.

8. Make changes to your financial plan. In light of vacillations in both your pay and your consumption, you ought to make changes to your spending plan.

9. Avoid making buys on impulse, since doing so may handily lose your monetary arrangement track. You ought to really bend over backward to avoid them.

10. Laying out an asset for unanticipated costs could assist you with meeting unforeseen costs and safeguard you from sliding into obligations.

11. Take advantage of limits and reserve funds. Amazing open doors by searching for coupons and limits that could be useful to you as you set aside cash.

12. Think about effective money management: Consider putting resources into stocks, securities, or other resources to help you reach your financial goals.

13. Plan a technique for the reimbursement of any obligations you might have. On the off chance that you have an obligation, figure out a procedure for taking care of it right away.

14. On the off chance that you want help, investigate recruiting a monetary counsellor or utilising a planning instrument. In the event that you're having issues fostering a spending plan or sticking to it, you could investigate recruiting help.

15. Perform ordinary surveys of your financial plan. You ought to perform routine audits of your financial plan to guarantee that it is still serving your requirements.

Chapter 3

Key 2: Live Inside Your Means

Keeping a spending plan that is sensible for your pay level is perhaps the main move towards achieving monetary security. It suggests not spending more cash than you get and placing the distinction into investment funds. This is a critical thought that might work with the most common way of gathering cash, wiping out obligations, and accomplishing freedom from one's monetary commitments.

Understanding both your pay and your uses is the most vital phase of living within your means. You should know about how much cash is streaming into your record every month as well as the sum that you are spending. You will actually want to develop a spending plan utilising this, as well as evaluate how much cash you have available to take care of. When you have a spending plan, you might start making changes so you can live within your means.

You might achieve this objective to some extent by eliminating your spending. Search for techniques to eliminate spending that isn't needed, and focus your consideration on the fundamentals. You might reduce expenses on the items you really want by searching for different techniques to set aside cash, for example, using coupons or doing examination shopping to get the best deals.

Expanding your income is another system you could use to live within your means. It's conceivable that this might require you to find a second line of work or send off a side business. You could likewise attempt to expand your compensation at your present place of employment by doing things like requesting a raise or taking on extra obligations at work.

Taking everything into account, you ought to focus on the formation of a backup stash. This is cash that you have saved if there should arise an occurrence of abrupt costs or other unforeseen occasions. In the event that something startling happens, having a bank account assigned for crises can assist you in trying not to fall into debt.

Keeping a degree of monetary security requires a way of life that is harmonious with one's assets. In spite of the fact that it requires restraint and devotion on your chapter, it can help you accumulate riches and achieve independence from your monetary commitments. You can start to live inside your means and recapture control of your funds once you have a strong comprehension of your pay and costs, have done whatever it may take to lessen those costs, have done whatever it takes to expand your pay, and have begun a secret stash.

Advantages Of Living Within Your Means

1. The capacity to fabricate a solid monetary future by living inside one's method: Building a protected monetary future requires living within one's means. You can set cash aside for various purposes, including retirement, spontaneous expenses, and different objectives.

2. Diminished degrees of stress: On the off chance that you don't need to fret over how you will take care of your bills since you're living within your means that is something less you need to stress over. Your general personal satisfaction may likewise improve, along with your feelings of anxiety.

3. A Better FICO Assessment: One of the advantages of spending less than what you acquire is an improvement score. Along these

lines, you might be qualified for lower rates of interest on advances and charge cards.

4. More prominent ability to save: When you spend short of what you procure every month, you have a more prominent ability to put cash down for what's in store. This might assist you with accomplishing your monetary targets in a more catalyst-like way.

5. More Prospects: You will actually want to make the most of a more noteworthy number of chances when you have cash saved. You might take an interest in yourself, send off an organisation, or travel with the cash.

6. At the point when you don't spend more than you get every month, you will not need to assume as much obligation to help your way of life. You might try not to get into serious

monetary challenges in the future because of this.

7. An expansion in one's feeling of satisfaction and fulfilment in oneself and one's accomplishments: This comes about when one lives within their monetary means. This could cause you to have good expectations about yourself.

8. Additional Time: When you are liberated from the pressure of stressing over cash, you have the chance to invest more energy by participating in exercises that give you pleasure. This might assist you with having an existence that is really fulfilling in general.

9. More prominent Monetary Adaptability: Assuming you deal with your spending so it doesn't surpass your pay, you will have more prominent monetary adaptability. This data

can help you make better choices with regards to your funds.

10. Further developed Connections: Since you don't need to fret over cash, you'll have the option to place a greater amount of your consideration into fortifying the bonds you share with your friends, family, and companions.

11. The capacity to be more liberal with one's cash when one lives inside one's method; when one does this, one can be more liberal with one's cash. You might make commitments to beneficent associations, help individuals from your own family, and put resources into the nearby local area.

12. More prominent Administer over Your Monetary Fate: You will have a more prominent capacity to control your monetary

future on the off chance that you live within your means. You can further develop the determinations that you make about how to spend your cash.

13. You can appreciate the everyday routine. More prominent when you experience life within your means, you can enjoy more of it. You are allowed to seek out exercises that give you pleasure regardless of monetary worries.

14. Living within your means takes into consideration. More inner harmony: Enjoying the harmony of the brain is conceivable when you live within your means. Since you are not worried about monetary issues, you are allowed to direct your focus towards different issues.

15. A Bigger Potential for Bliss: In the event that you live within your means, you might find that you experience more satisfaction. You don't have to let worries about cash keep you from appreciating life.

Chapter 4

Key 3: Pay down Obligation

Many individuals observe that their obligations are a critical wellspring of both pressure and uneasiness in their lives. Taking care of obligations is a fundamental chapter of achieving monetary steadiness, and doing so can likewise help alleviate pressure and improve, generally speaking, monetary wellbeing.

Making a spending plan is the main thing you ought to do while attempting to escape obligation. This will assist with distinguishing regions in which cash is being spent unnecessarily as well as regions in which more cash can be apportioned towards the reimbursement of obligations. It is fundamental to maintain cautious records of all uses as well as pay to ensure that the financial plan is precise and state-of-the-art.

After a financial plan has been laid out, taking care of obligations ought to be at the top of the list of needs. To achieve this, you ought to concentrate completely on taking care of the obligation that conveys the most noteworthy loan cost first, as this will bring about the best, generally speaking, monetary reserve funds over the long haul.

Moreover, it is fundamental to verify that all base instalments are made on time, as instalments that are made late can bring about extra expenses and financing costs that are higher.

It is crucial to search for ways of eliminating obligations as well as making the necessary instalments on a predictable basis. This might include haggling with banks for lower financing costs or uniting different obligations into a single credit. Then again, it might include taking care of numerous obligations at the same time. It is fundamental that you avoid assuming any new obligation whatsoever, as this will just build up your general obligation trouble.

Taking everything into account, it is basic to guarantee that there is cash saved for unforeseen costs. This will assist with guaranteeing that unexpected costs can be covered without depending on Mastercards or different types of obligations if they emerge. If an unforeseen cost emerges, having a backup stash can assist with lessening pressure and giving true serenity, which are both very useful.

Taking care of obligations is a fundamental chapter of achieving monetary strength, and doing so may likewise help with alleviating pressure and improving, generally speaking, monetary wellbeing. It is possible to gain ground towards a future in which one has no monetary commitments by laying out a spending plan, making the decrease and reimbursement of obligations one's first concern, and looking for extra techniques to set aside cash. If an unanticipated need emerges, bringing a rainy day account previously settled may help to the table for inner harmony and diminish the probability that you should rely upon credit to take care of the expense.

Kinds of obligation

There are only a couple sorts of obligations portrayed here, and they are as per the following:

1. An obligation gathered by a client because of the use of a Mastercard to make an acquisition of labour and products is referred to as a charge card obligation.

2. Understudy loan obligation is the obligation that is produced when an understudy applies for a new line of credit to pay for schooling costs and different consumptions related to going to school.

3. An obligation caused by a borrower because they applied for a line of credit to buy a property is referred to as a home loan obligation.

4. An obligation gained because a borrower has applied for a new line of credit to buy a vehicle is referred to as a car credit obligation.

5. Obligation from individual credits is how much cash is out and owed by a borrower credit for their very own utilisation.

6. Obligation Got through Business Credits: This sort of obligation is produced when an organisation gets a credit to help either their tasks or their development.

7. Payday credit obligation otherwise called a payday advance obligation, this sort of obligation is created when a borrower takes out a momentary advance that has exorbitant financing costs.

8. Charge Obligation: The monetary commitment that results when a citizen is late

in the instalment of expenses that are attributable to the public authority.

9. Clinical Obligation: The monetary commitment that results when a patient can't pay for the clinical medicines they have gotten.

10. An obligation caused by a borrower to apply for a new line of credit against the value of their home is referred to as a home value advance obligation.

11. House Value Credit Extension Obligation (HELOC Obligation): Obligation that a borrower causes when they apply for a new line of credit against the value of their home.

12. An obligation that is gotten by guarantee, like a vehicle or a house, is alluded to as a got obligation.

13. Debt without collateral, in some cases referred to as uncollateralized debt, will be an obligation that isn't upheld by any sort of security and is, for the most chapter, harder to obtain.

14. The obligation committed by individuals to acquire labour and products is referred to as the buyer obligation.

15. In business speech, "business obligation" alludes to obligations acquired to make acquisitions of items and services.

16. Obligation Got by the Public Authority: Obligation Procured by the Public Authority to Buy Labour and Products

17. An obligation brought about by unfamiliar substances to buy labour and products is referred to as an unfamiliar obligation.

18. A convertible obligation is an obligation that, at the choice of the loan specialist, might be changed into value.

19. In finance, "garbage obligation" alludes to an obligation that is viewed as being of low quality and involves a high possibility of defaulting on instalments.

20. In finance, a subordinate is an obligation instrument whose worth is determined in view of that of a fundamental resource or security.

Procedures For Settling Obligations

The weight of one's obligations might be a huge reason for mental misery as well as monetary precarity. With regards to wiping out obligations and laying out one's position in the monetary world, it is generally difficult to decide how to get everything rolling. Next up is a rundown of 15 different ways that might help you pay off your obligations and achieve monetary dependability:

1. Foster a spending plan or spending plan. Fostering a spending plan is the most vital phase in meeting obligations and achieving monetary security. Making a financial plan will empower you to monitor your pay and spending, as well as regions in which you might make decreases.

2. Monitor your spending. It is vital to monitor your spending whenever you have a financial

plan, so make certain to do so. This will help you recognise regions in which you are causing pointless consumption, with the goal that you can make fitting changes.

3. Form a procedure for the compensation of your obligation. Whenever you have decided the regions in which you might make decreases, the next stage is to plan a technique for the reimbursement of your obligation. This methodology needs to contain a plan for when you will take care of every obligation, along with a gauge of the sum that you will pay every month.

4. Focus on the instalment of obligations. Focusing on the instalment of obligations is basic. The obligation with the best loan fee ought to be taken care of first, followed by the obligation with the following most elevated rate, etc.

5. Make extra instalments: Assuming you have additional cash accessible, make additional instalments on your obligation. You will actually want to take care of your obligation all the more rapidly and get a good deal on interest instalments in the event that you do this.

6. Solidify your obligations: On the off chance that you have various credits, you could contemplate joining them into a solitary advance. Accordingly, the method involved with reimbursing your obligation will turn out to be not so convoluted but rather more reasonable for you.

7. Speak with your liabilities. In the event that you are experiencing difficulty making your bills, you ought to reach out to your loan bosses and check whether they are prepared

to arrange a diminished financing cost or an instalment plan with you.

8. Utilise an equilibrium move: On the off chance that you have a Mastercard obligation with an exorbitant loan cost, you ought to contemplate moving the sum to a card with a decreased loan cost. You will actually want to take care of your obligation all the more rapidly and get a good deal on interest instalments in the event that you do this.

9. Consider having a subsequent work: On the off chance that you have any extra time to burn, you could ponder getting a second vocation to help you take care of your obligations all the more rapidly.

10. Take stock of your stuff and sell any products that you never again need or use. This is a decent chance to get some additional money. You will actually want to procure more

income accordingly, which you might spend towards the reimbursement of your obligation.

11. Diminish spending on things that aren't in any way required: Glance through your financial plan cautiously and select any spending that isn't exactly important that you can decrease. Along these lines, you will actually want to let loose more assets to go towards the reimbursement of your obligation.

12. Exploit charge derivations: Assuming that you are now making instalments on any type of obligation, including understudy loans or different kinds of obligations, you might be entitled to charge allowances. Guarantee that you exploit these derivations so you might bring down how much cash you owe in charges.

13. Consider getting the help of an expert on the off chance that you are experiencing difficulty staying aware of the administration of your obligation. A monetary consultant or credit advisor might help you form a system for taking care of your obligations and give direction on the most proficient method to more readily deal with your cash generally.

14. Keep your inspiration up, since taking care of obligations might be a long and testing task. It is fundamental to keep up with your inspiration and remain focused on the system you made to take care of your obligations.

15. Lay out an asset for startling costs: After you have fulfilled your monetary commitments, the subsequent stage is to lay out an asset for surprising costs. You will not need to stress over falling into obligations later on in the

event that you find these ways to be prepared for unforeseen expenses.

You might pay off your obligation and lay out monetary solidity in the event that you follow these strategies and set them in motion. It is conceivable that it might require some investment and work; however, in the end, it will definitely be justified.

Chapter 5

Key 4: Form A Secret Stash.

Laying out a possible investment account is a significant step towards achieving monetary security. A bank account that is explicitly assigned for taking care of unanticipated expenses, for example, those related to losing one's employment, causing unforeseen doctor's visit expenses, or expecting to have significant auto fixes, is known as a secret stash.

At the point when a surprising need comes up, having an investment account assigned for crises could assist you with abstaining from venturing into the red or getting cash from direct relations and companions.

The primary thing you want to do to set up a secret stash is to ascertain how much cash you should save. The standard proposal among monetary counsellors is to have three to a half years of living costs buried in a backup stash. This shows that you ought to have sufficient cash saved to meet your necessary requirements for three to a half years, including your lease, utilities, food, and transportation.

The next stage, in the wake of deciding how much cash you want to take care of in reserve funds, is to figure out how you will take care of that cash. To begin, make a spending plan and make slices for things that aren't in any way required. Along these lines, you will actually want to save more cash in your bank account for unexpected costs. You could likewise look for different strategies to raise your pay, for example, getting seasonal work or selling stuff that you never use again. Both of these choices are feasible choices.

You will actually want to begin putting something aside for your secret stash when you have an arrangement for your funds and extra pay. It is crucial to verify that your reserve funds are kept in an area that is both secure and helpful to get to when essential. You will actually want to bring in a higher premium on your cash in the event that you save it in a high-return investment account, which is a fabulous decision to consider.

All in all, it is vital to remember that the foundation of a backup stash is a cycle that requires some investment. It is conceivable that it might require some investment for you to set aside how much cash you want; along these lines, it is fundamental that you keep up with your inspiration and monitor your advancement. You may likewise set aside standard instalments in your investment account by sorting out assets to be sent from your financial records on a foreordained timetable. This will guarantee that you generally have cash saved.

Laying out a possible bank account is a significant step towards achieving monetary security. If an unexpected consumption emerges, it might help you try not to venture into the red and proposition you with a piece of brain. You might get an early advantage on developing a backup stash immediately in the event that you make a spending plan, work on developing your pay, and set aside cash in a record that offers a high rate of return.

Advantages Of A Secret Stash

1. Genuine serenity with regards to your funds: Having a backup stash might give you genuine serenity with regards to your funds in the event of a startling use or loss of pay. It can possibly save you from falling into debt or being compelled to rely upon Mastercards or advances to meet your monetary commitments.

2. True serenity: Having a secret stash might furnish you with the true serenity that comes from realising that you have a monetary cradle to depend on in case of a surprising situation. This might assist with limiting sensations of stress and worry around unanticipated monetary commitments.

3. Assists Defend Your Credit with scoring: A backup stash provides you with a wellspring

of money that you might use to cover unexpected bills, so you don't need to rely on Visas or advances to compensate for any shortfall. This can assist with safeguarding your FICO assessment.

4. Helps You in Avoiding Exorbitant Premium Obligation: Having a secret stash might help you in avoiding exorbitant premium obligation by providing you with a wellspring of money that you can use to cover unexpected consumptions, so you don't need to rely upon Visas or credits.

5. Helps You in Accomplishing Your Monetary Objectives: A backup stash might help you in accomplishing your monetary objectives by giving you access to a wellspring of money that can be utilised to pay for unforeseen expenses, so you are not compelled to rely upon charge cards or credits.

6. You'll have a Wellspring of Money to Cover Unanticipated Consumptions. A secret stash provides you with a wellspring of assets that you can use to cover unforeseen costs, so you don't need to rely on Mastercards or credits to do so. This assists you with setting aside cash.

7. It helps you adhere to your spending plan. A backup stash might help you adhere to your financial plan by giving you a wellspring of money that can be used to take care of unexpected expenses, so you don't need to rely on Mastercards or credits.

8. You'll have a Wellspring of Money to Cover Unanticipated Consumptions Having a backup stash provides you with a wellspring of assets that you can use to pay unforeseen costs, so you don't need to rely on visas or

credits to cover them. This assists you in trying not to make superfluous purchases.

9. Helps You in Preparing for Unforeseen Expenses: Having a backup stash might help you in preparing for unexpected expenses by giving you a wellspring of money that you can use to meet these expenses without relying upon Visas or different types of cash.

10. You'll have a wellspring of money to take care of unanticipated costs. A backup stash provides you with a wellspring of assets that you can use to cover startling costs, so you don't need to rely on charge cards or credits to pay for them. This wipes out the requirement for you to pay late charges.

11. Can Assist You with Keeping Away from Insolvency: Having a backup stash can assist you with trying not to become bankrupt since

it provides you with a wellspring of cash that you can use to cover unexpected bills without utilising charge cards or taking out credits.

12. Helps You in Enduring Monetary Tempests: A backup stash might help you in enduring monetary tempests by furnishing you with a wellspring of cash to meet unexpected expenses, so you don't need to rely upon Mastercards or credits to compensate for any shortfall.

13. It might assist you with remaining focused. A backup stash can assist you with remaining focused on your monetary targets by giving you a wellspring of cash to meet unanticipated expenses, so you don't need to rely upon Mastercards or credits to compensate for any shortfall.

14. Helps You in Financial Planning: A secret stash might help you in effective money management by providing you with a wellspring of cash to meet unexpected expenses, so you don't need to rely upon Mastercards or credits.

15. Helps You in Accomplishing Monetary Freedom: A backup stash might help you achieve monetary freedom by giving you a wellspring of money that can be used to cover unanticipated consumptions without expecting you to depend on Mastercards or different types of obligations.

The Most Effective Method To Make A Rainy Day Account

1. Describe what you need to achieve with your Rainy Day account. You ought to initially determine how much cash you need to have buried in a just-in-case account before you begin setting aside cash for what's in store. A decent guideline to keep is to pursue the objective of having set aside three to a half years of one's everyday costs.

2. Lay out a different investment account from your other monetary records as a whole. Make another investment account that is different from the ones you currently have and is simply equipped to fill in as a secret stash. It will be a lot less complex for you to keep your backup stash separate from your other reserve funds and spending accounts on the off

chance that you coordinate your funds along these lines.

3. Robotize your reserve funds. By setting up programmed moves, you might move cash from your financial records to the record you use to put something aside for surprising necessities. Since doing so will permit you to spend less cash, you won't actually have to really think about it.

4. Begin with a Minuscule Sum When you first start, begin with a limited quantity, for example, $50 or $100 each month. This will assist you with getting the hang of things. It is feasible for you to expand the sum that you set aside into reserve funds in direct proportion to the development of your pay.

5. Give your monetary stores first concern. Laying out a crisis reserve fund pad ought to continuously overshadow the quest for some

other monetary objectives you might have. In the event that you do this, you will actually want to build up how much cash is in your secret stash all the more quickly.

6. Regularly practice it: Make it a highlight, put away some cash consistently for your potential asset, and regularly practice it as such. Put a note in your telephone or on your schedule to remind you to contribute cash to your backup stash consistently. The fact that you do this makes it proposed.

7. Scale Back Your Uses to take care of more money for a possibility reserve, you ought to search for ways of scaling back your flow consumption.

8. Capitalise on Surprising Cash: Assuming you are sufficiently fortunate to get a reward or an expense form, go through that cash towards

building your investment funds so you are ready for any unanticipated conditions that might emerge.

9. Watch Your Headway Keep a close eye on how far along you are currently in achieving your objective for your secret stash. This will assist with keeping you persuaded and on target to accomplish the goals that you have set for yourself.

10. Utilise records that give tax breaks. You ought to consider using charge-advantaged records, for example, a Singular Retirement Record (IRA) or a Wellbeing Bank account (HSA), while you are trying to set aside cash for a secret stash. These are two instances of records (HSA).

11. Think about putting after you have set aside sufficient cash to cover your costs for three to

a half years of everyday costs, you ought to genuinely consider putting your secret stash into a generally safe venture.

12. Try not to contact your Rainy Day account until you've collected sufficient cash to cover startling costs! At the point when you have sufficient cash to put something aside for a secret stash, you shouldn't get to it for any uses that aren't crises since you shouldn't contact it until you have sufficient cash to put something aside for a just-in-case account.

13. Continuously watch out for the amount you have saved. Lay out a daily practice of standardising your assets to see whether they keep on being adequate to fulfil your necessities in the event of an emergency. Make it a highlight. Do this as frequently as could be expected.

14. Rebalance the Asset That You Have You
ought to continually make it a highlight to
rebalance your secret stash whenever there is
an adjustment to either your pay or your
costs.

15. Investigate your monetary stores. You ought
to do an evaluation of your reserve funds
consistently to see whether they keep
satisfying your requirements if a surprising
consumption emerges.

Chapter 6

Key 5: Contribute For Retirement

It is crucial to get ready for retirement to ensure what is going on will stay stable all through this huge life-altering situation. Putting cash down for your older years through ventures is one of the best procedures for guaranteeing that you will have the assets to partake in an agreeable way of life when that opportunity arrives. Putting resources into one's retirement might be a nerve-wracking experience; in any case, on the off chance that one is outfitted with the fitting data and devices, the cycle can be both fulfilling and peaceful.

Picking what you believe your retirement should resemble is the most important phase of the time spent putting something aside for it. Do you have desires to go on excursions, purchase houses, or simply continue to experience the manner in which you do now? How much cash you want to save and how you need to contribute it are still up in the air, to some degree, based on the goals you have set for yourself. At the point when you have an unmistakable idea of what you need to achieve, you can begin exploring the numerous sorts of speculations accessible to you.

Stocks, securities, common assets, and annuities are the four principal types of speculations that individuals make for their retirement reserve funds. Due to the likelihood that their worth might ascend with the progression of time, stocks are a great venture vehicle for achieving long-term gains. Bonds are a safer option than stocks because of the way that they turn out a set amount of revenue and are less liable to cost changes. Shared reserves are a sort of speculation vehicle that joins stocks and bonds into an enhanced portfolio determined to relieve monetary risk. An annuity is a particular sort of insurance policy that might ensure a specific amount of cash consistently after retirement.

Prior to taking on any type of monetary responsibility, it is essential to have a strong comprehension of the risks that are innate to that specific speculation. Taking into account the vulnerability and unconventionality of the securities exchange, putting resources into stocks may be viewed as a high-risk movement. Bonds are often seen as a safer venture decision; in any case, it is conceivable that they may not convey the same measure of development as values. Individuals who wish to expand their resources might need to think about shared assets as another option; in any case, financial backers ought to know that common subsidies accompany their own special arrangement of risks. Annuities can ensure a specific degree of pay forever; however, not every person has a decent possibility for them.

While arranging your ventures for retirement, it is fundamental to assess both your comfort level with risk and how much time you have available. On the off chance that you are a financial backer who holds speculations for a more drawn-out timeframe, you might be prepared to acknowledge a more prominent degree of hazard to procure greater returns. Assuming you are simply keen on making speculations for the present moment, you ought to presumably focus on additional moderate choices that give predictable returns. It is additionally vital to ponder how old you are and how much longer you should work prior to resigning. At the point when you're more youthful, you have additional opportunity to contribute, and you're more able to face challenges than when you're more seasoned.

All in all, with regards to putting something aside for retirement, it is fundamental to talk with a monetary guide. Your targets, your degree of solace with risk, and the time span you have available to put may be generally included in a redone methodology with the help of a monetary counsellor. They are likewise ready to give you direction on the resources that are generally reasonable for your conditions and help you keep a reliable reserve fund plan for your retirement.

Contributing for retirement might be a difficult undertaking, but by and by, on the off chance that one is furnished with the essential abilities and instruments, the interaction can be both fulfilling and peaceful. You might ensure that you will have sufficient cash to carry on with an agreeable life all through your retirement years by obviously characterising your goals, monitoring the dangers that are associated with the different speculations you make, and working with a monetary counsellor.

Advantages Of Effective Money Management For Retirement

1. Investing for retirement might bring tax reductions, for example, charge-conceded development, and that implies that you will not need to pay charges on the cash you contribute until you really eliminate it from the record. This is one of the essential benefits of retirement. You might have the option to take care of more cash for your retirement, assuming you do this.

2. Accumulate Revenue: Setting aside cash for retirement could assist you with exploiting build revenue, which is the point at which you bring in revenue on the cash you've recently procured as well as revenue on the cash you've previously acquired. This might assist your assets for retirement by expanding at a more rapid rate.

3. Expansion: Putting aside for retirement might help you enhance your resources, which can help decrease the probability of you causing monetary misfortune.

4. Admittance to Proficient Insight and Direction: Contributing for retirement might give you admittance to proficient exhortation and heading, the two of which can help you in pursuing taught decisions about your speculations.

5. Pay in Retirement: Putting resources into your retirement might assist you with creating a persistent kind of revenue in retirement, which can assist you with keeping up with the way of life you've been used to all through your functioning years.

6. Putting resources into retirement might assist you with building a protected retirement and

give you true serenity. Putting resources into retirement can assist you with making a safe retirement, which can give you inner harmony.

7. Reserve funds for as long as possible. Putting resources into retirement might help you put something aside for as long as possible, which can help you accomplish your retirement targets.

8. Putting resources into retirement might give you adaptability in the way you spend your retirement reserves, for example, the capacity to pull out cash for an excursion or a home fix project. This can be a huge advantage for retirement contributions.

9. Keeping Up with Command over Your Retirement Reserve Funds Putting resources into your retirement might help you keep up

with command over your retirement reserve funds, which can help you guarantee that your cash is spent on the things that you want.

10. Reserve funds for retirement: Putting resources into your retirement will assist you with setting aside more cash for retirement, which can help you accomplish your retirement targets.

11. Putting resources into your retirement will help you anticipate your retirement, which can help you guarantee that you have the assets to persevere during your retirement.

12. Assurance of Your Retirement Reserve Funds Putting resources into your retirement might assist you with protecting your retirement reserve funds, which can thus assist you with guaranteeing that your cash is secure.

13. Putting resources into retirement might assist you with building your reserve funds for retirement. Putting resources into retirement can assist you with developing your investment funds for retirement, which can assist you with having more cash in retirement.

14. Retirement Genuine serenity: Putting resources into your retirement will assist you with experiencing retirement harmony of psyche, which will permit you to partake in your retirement years more.

15. Leaving a Heritage through Retirement Investment Funds: Assuming you set aside cash for your retirement, you might leave an inheritance for your family that will assist them with having a more steady monetary future.

Kinds Of Retirement Accounts

1. Customary Individual Retirement Record (IRA): A conventional individual retirement account (IRA) is a sort of retirement investment account that empowers people to make commitments with pre-charged dollars and delay paying duties on those commitments until the assets are removed during retirement.

2. Roth Individual Retirement Record (IRA): A Roth IRA is a sort of retirement bank account that empowers people to make commitments with cash that has proactively been burdened and afterward take that cash in retirement without being liable to additional charges.

3. 401(k): A 401(k), otherwise called a certified retirement investment funds plan, is a reserve funds program that is supported by a

business. It offers labourers the chance to contribute cash before charges are removed from it, and it empowers businesses to match their commitments.

4. 403(b): A 403(b) is an investment fund plan for retirement that is presented by an association that isn't for-benefit. It offers labourers the chance to contribute cash before charges are removed from it, and it empowers managers to match their commitments.

5. SEP IRA: A SEP IRA is a sort of individual retirement account (IRA) that empowers individuals who are independently employed or who own a small organisation to make commitments utilising pre-charged cash and to get charge-conceded development on those commitments.

6. Basic Individual Retirement Record (Straightforward IRA): A straightforward IRA is a singular retirement account that is planned for use by small undertakings with less than 100 specialists. It offers labourers the chance to contribute cash before charges are removed from it, and it empowers managers to match their commitments.

7. Solo 401(k): A Solo 401(k) is a sort of retirement investment fund plan that was developed explicitly for individuals who are independently employed or who own private ventures. They will actually want to contribute cash before charges are removed from it, and their manager will contribute an equivalent sum.

8. Annuity An annuity is an agreement that is made between an individual and an insurance agency. It provides the individual with the

choice of making one enormous instalment or numerous more modest instalments throughout the span of time as a trade-off for a constant flow of guaranteed pay in retirement.

9. Benefits: An annuity is a reserve fund programme for retirement that is presented by a business. It prepares labourers to get a constant flow of guaranteed pay once they resign.

10. A consolidated remuneration plan is a business-supported retirement reserve fund plan. A conceded pay plan is a sort of retirement reserve fund plan that is supported by a business. It offers labourers the chance to put off paying charges on a piece of their compensation in return for development that isn't dependent upon tax collection.

11. Benefit Sharing Arrangement. A business could support a retirement investment fund plan known as a benefit-sharing arrangement for its workers. It offers businesses the chance to give a portion of their income to the retirement records of their labourers.

12. Cash Buy Plan An organisation might uphold a representative's cooperation in a cash buy plan, which is a sort of retirement reserve fund plan. It enables organisations to contribute a foreordained measure of cash to the retirement records of their labourers.

13. A frugality investment fund plan, sometimes known as a TSP, is an arrangement for setting aside cash for retirement that is supported by the central government. Commitments made by government labourers might be made utilizing cash that has previously been

burdened, and any development in the record isn't dependent upon tax assessment.

14. Non-Qualified Conceded Remuneration Plan. A business-supported retirement investment fund plan is referred to as a non-qualified conceded pay plan. It offers labourers the chance to put off paying charges on a piece of their compensation in return for development that isn't dependent upon tax collection.

15. Individual Retirement Record (IRA): A singular retirement account (IRA) is a sort of investment account for retirement that empowers individuals to make commitments utilising cash that has previously been burdened and to appreciate development on those supports tax-exempt.

Chapter 7

Key 6: Put resources into protection.

It is crucial for one's monetary security to have interests in different kinds of protection. Protection is a sort of monetary security that defends an individual's funds on account of unanticipated conditions like disorder, inadequacy, or passing. It is likewise feasible for it to provide insurance against the monetary misfortunes that are connected with the harm done to property, liabilities, and different risks.

Your property and your family's monetary prosperity may both benefit from the security managed by insurance contracts. It could be useful in covering consumptions related to unanticipated occasions, including medical clinic bills, entombment expenses, and different charges that might be caused by the event. Protection may likewise help with covering the costs associated with legitimate bills, harm to property, and different sorts of misfortunes.

You can all the more likely arrangement for the future with the help of protection. It is feasible for it to give you the true serenity that comes from realising that you are financially prepared for any unexpected events that might occur. You might be qualified for charge derivations and different advantages, assuming that you have protection, the two of which might assist you with setting aside cash.

Protection is another device that could help you shield your cash. Conceivable, doing so would help you defend your cash from monetary misfortunes caused by changes on the lookout or different perils. Protection may likewise help you safeguard your resources from extra dangers and risks, like burglary and misrepresentation.

Protection is another device that could help you safeguard your organization. It might protect you against monetary harm that might happen because of representative indiscretion, item responsibility, and other likely risks. Buying protection may likewise help you safeguard your organisation from different perils and lawful commitments.

Your family is one more significant gathering to shield with protection and inclusion. You may be safeguarded against the monetary misfortunes that are connected with death, incapacity, and infection with the assistance of this sort of protection. You may likewise safeguard your family monetarily against the potential monetary misfortunes that are connected with property harm, liabilities, and different perils by buying protection.

Having sufficient protection is one of the most mind-blowing ways to shield your monetary prosperity. It can possibly both shield your funds against unexpected events and help you bring down your large monetary costs. Moreover, it might help you safeguard your family as well as your cash and your organization. You might better prepare for the future by putting resources into protection, which is a fundamental chapter of keeping up with your monetary security.

Kinds Of Protection

1. Disaster protection: Life coverage is a kind of insurance contract that, on account of the policyholder's passing, gives the recipients monetary security. If the policyholder dies, it makes a one-time instalment to the recipients as a protuberance sum.

2. Health care coverage: Health care coverage is a particular kind of insurance contract that repays policyholders for the costs caused while getting clinical treatment. It very well might be used to help with paying for outings to the specialist, stays in the clinic, doctor-prescribed drugs, and different sorts of clinical expenses.

3. Collision protection: Accident protection is a
    sort of property and setback protection that
    safeguards policyholders monetarily if they are
    engaged in a mishap or experience another
    kind of harm to their vehicle. It could be
    useful in paying for fixes, clinical costs, and
    different expenses connected with a mishap
    that you might have brought about.

4. Mortgage Holders Insurance: Property
    Holders Protection is a particular sort of
    protection contract that offers policyholders
    monetary security if their home or property
    supports harm. It could be useful in paying
    for fixes, clinical costs, and different expenses
    connected with a mishap that you might have
    brought about.

5. Handicap Insurance: Incapacity protection is a
    kind of protection contract that offers

policyholders monetary security if they become unfit to work because of a disease or injury covered by the contract. It very well may be useful in covering doctor's visit expenses, compensation lost because of disease or injury, and different expenses related to the condition.

6. Long-haul Care Insurance: Long-haul care protection is a kind of protection contract that gives monetary security to policyholders in case of a drawn-out sickness or injury that requires long-haul care. This security can be utilised if the policyholder needs long-haul care for a drawn-out timeframe. Long-haul care costs, for example, those caused in nursing homes and at home, can be to some degree or completely covered by this sort of protection.

7. Risk Insurance: Obligation protection is a kind of protection contract that gives monetary security to policyholders in case of a mishap or other harm brought about by the policyholder's carelessness or deliberate demonstrations. This assurance can be used if the policyholder is seen as lawfully liable for the mishap or harm. It is workable for it to help with paying for lawful charges, doctor's visit expenses, and different costs that are related to a mishap.

8. Property Insurance: Property protection is a particular sort of protection contract that offers policyholders monetary security if harm is done to their property. It very well might be useful in paying for fixes, the cost of supplanting harmed property, and different consumptions connected with property harm.

9. Business Protection: Business protection is a particular sort of protection inclusion that offers monetary security to organisations if they are engaged in a mishap or experience different kinds of mischief because of their own thoughtlessness or intentional activities. It is workable for it to help with paying for legal costs, hospital expenses, and different consumptions that are associated with a mishap.

10. Travel Protection: Travel protection is a particular sort of protection inclusion that safeguards voyagers monetarily if they are engaged in a mishap or experience another sort of damage because of their own thoughtlessness or intentional activities. It might help with the instalment of charges like doctor's visit expenses, lost stuff, and different costs.

11. Pet Protection: Pet protection is a sort of property and setback protection that safeguards the monetary prosperity of pet people if their creatures are engaged in a mishap or cause different kinds of damage. It could be utilised to aid in the instalment of veterinarian charges, hospital expenses, and some other expenses connected with a mishap.

12. Flood Insurance: Flood protection is a particular sort of protection contract that offers policyholders monetary security if they are exposed to floods. It could be useful in paying for consumptions connected with floods, like fixes and substitutions, as well as different expenses.

13. Quake Insurance: Seismic tremor protection is a particular type of protection contract that offers policyholders monetary security on account of a catastrophic event like a tremor.

It is conceivable that it might help pay for fixes, costs associated with substitution, and different uses connected with a quake.

14. Insurance against Wholesale Fraud Data fraud protection is a particular sort of protection contract that offers policyholders monetary security if their own data is stolen. It very well might be useful in covering legitimate bills, checking credit, and different costs associated with data fraud.

15. Credit Insurance: Credit protection is a kind of protection contract that offers policyholders monetary security if they neglect to reimburse a credit or other type of obligation as settled upon in the contract. It is workable for it to help pay for lawful costs, gathering charges, and different costs that are connected with a default.

16. Digital insurance is a type of protection contract that offers monetary security for policyholders on account of a digital assault or other information breach. Digital protection may likewise be referred to as advanced protection. It might help with taking care of lawful bills, accusations related to information recuperation, and different consumptions that are engaged in a digital attack.

17. Labourers' Remuneration Protection: Labourers' pay protection is a type of protection inclusion that offers financial security to organisations if a worker has an infcction or mishap while at work. It could have the option to help with paying for extra consumption related to a mishap or affliction, like missed pay and doctor's visit expenses.

18. Proficient Obligation Protection: Proficient risk protection is a kind of protection inclusion that safeguards experts monetarily if

they commit an error or are careless in the presentation of their business. It could be utilised to help with taking care of lawful bills, harms, and different expenses connected with a blunder or careless demonstration.

19. Marine Insurance: Marine protection is a kind of protection contract that offers policyholders monetary security on account of a misfortune or harm to a vessel or freight. This security may be money-related remuneration. It very well might be useful in paying for fixes, accusations involved in substitution, and different consumptions related to a misfortune or harm.

20. Flight Insurance: Flying protection is a particular sort of protection contract that offers policyholders monetary security if an aeroplane is lost or harmed. It could be useful in paying for fixes, accusations involved in

substitution, and different consumptions related to a misfortune or harm.

Advantages Of Protection

1. True serenity and monetary security: Protection might give inner harmony and monetary security by safeguarding you and your family from the potential monetary misfortunes that may be caused by an unanticipated event.

2. Risk The board: Protection is a powerful apparatus for risk managers since it permits the guaranteed to move their gamble to the guarantor. This assists with protecting you against monetary harm that can be caused by something totally surprising.

3. Tax breaks numerous protection plans accompany tax reductions that could help you bring down how much cash you owe in charges.

4. An instrument for effective financial planning, insurance contracts may likewise be utilised in this limit. They guarantee that you will get a profit from your speculation come what may, which could help you hoard cash over the long haul.

5. Anticipating Retirement: Protection inclusion might be utilised during the time spent on retirement planning. They turn out a surefire revenue stream that could help you keep up with your way of life whenever you reach retirement age.

6. Making an Arrangement for Your Domain Insurance Contracts might be utilised to help with the security of your home and to ensure that your friends and family will be accommodated following your passing.

7. Gives true serenity. Having protection might give you an inward feeling of harmony since it safeguards you and your family from monetary misfortunes that might be caused by an unanticipated episode.

8. Resource Security: On the off chance that you are engaged in a claim or some other sort of lawful activity, having protection might help safeguard your resources from being taken from you.

9. Cost reserve funds: In the event that you have protection, you might lessen how much cash you need to spend on things like clinical uses, fixes to damaged property, and different kinds of misfortunes.

10. Inclusion for Unexpected Events: Protection might provide inclusion for occasions that are not covered by different types of protection,

like catastrophic events or demonstrations of psychological oppression. This is a huge benefit of having protection.

11. Protection plans might be altered to match the singular necessities of every client and their monetary imperatives.

12. Admittance to skill protection firms gives their clients admittance to learned individuals who can direct them through the method involved with pursuing instructed decisions about their protection inclusion.

13. Making a Monetary Arrangement Protection might help you in making a monetary arrangement for the future by giving a consistent wellspring of ensured pay and by helping you in the collection of abundance over the long run.

14. Inward feeling of harmony: Experiencing protection might give you harmony of the brain since it safeguards you and your family from the potential monetary harms that could result from an unanticipated event.

15. Inner harmony: Having protection gives you and your family the genuine serenity that comes from realising that you are safeguarded against the potential monetary harms that may be welcomed by an unanticipated disaster.

Chapter 8

Key 7: Monitor Your Credit

Having a safe monetary establishment is a fundamental chapter of a satisfying life. It is crucial to know about your FICO rating and to keep close track of it on a reliable basis. This might help you guarantee that you are in a solid monetary position and can help you settle on better decisions about your funds.

Your record as a consumer is the essential element that contributes to the computation of your three-digit FICO rating. Moneylenders will take a gander at it to assess how likely it is that you will actually want to reimburse a credit. In the event that you have a superior FICO rating, it is more likely that monetary establishments will give you credit when you apply for an advance or a Mastercard. In the event that you have an unfortunate FICO rating, you risk not being supported for a credit or charge card.

Keeping up with your monetary security requires that you watch out for your credit report. It is fundamental to keep a routine eye on your credit report to guarantee that it is free from any missteps or different sorts of incorrect data. You ought to likewise look at your FICO rating to guarantee that it gives an exact impression of your monetary standing. Assuming you uncover any slip-ups or disparities on your credit report, you ought to reach out to the credit authority so they might be fixed.

It is fundamental that you watch out for your credit report for any signs that your character might have been taken. In the event that you run into any problematic conduct on your credit report, you ought to reach out to the acknowledgement department as well as the specialists right away.

Keeping up with your monetary security requires that you watch out for your credit report. It is fundamental to do routine checks of both your credit report and financial assessment to guarantee that neither contains any slip-ups or incorrect data. It is fundamental that you watch out for your credit report for any signs that your personality might have been taken. Assuming you watch out for your credit report, you can assist with ensuring what is happening is steady and that you can make sound decisions about your cash.

Advantages Of Checking Your Credit

1. Safeguards against Wholesale Fraud Credit observing may assist you with distinguishing any uncommon way of behaving or unlawful utilisation of your own data, which can shield you from the possibly destroying impacts of wholesale fraud. This data might help you make an earnest move to protect both your prosperity and your monetary circumstances.

2. It helps you distinguish issues. Credit checking may help you identify mistakes on your credit report that might be affecting your financial assessment in a bad way.

3. It helps you monitor your advancement. Credit observation can help you monitor your advancement as you endeavour to build your FICO rating.

4. Keeping up with the Control of Your Monetary Circumstance Credit observing can help you keep track of your monetary circumstances by informing you of any changes made to either your FICO assessment or your credit report.

5. You will be informed when your equilibrium is low. Observing can tell you when your equilibrium is getting low, which will assist you in trying not to overdraft expenses.

6. Works on Your Possibilities Getting better financing costs Credit checking can work on your possibilities of acquiring better financing costs on advances and Mastercards by informing you of expansions in your FICO rating.

7. Builds Your Possibilities Being Supported for Advances Credit checking can expand your

possibilities of having credit applications endorsed by telling you at whatever point your financial assessment goes up.

8. You will be cautious of any dubious movement on your credit report. Credit observing can assist you with keeping away from misrepresentation by informing you in advance of any action on your credit report that seems, by all accounts, to be dubious.

9. Checking your credit can help you observe your MasterCard movement. Credit checking can help you check your Visa action by advising you of any possibly deceitful action.

10. It assists you with watching out for the amount of your accessible credit. You're Utilising Credit-Observing Administrations can help you monitor the amount of accessible credit you're utilising by sending

you warnings when your equilibrium gets excessively high.

11. It assists you with monitoring your obligations. Credit observing may help you in monitoring your obligation by advising you when the sum for you has arrived at a perilous level.

12. It assists you with monitoring requests made to your credit report. Credit checking might be useful to you in monitoring requests made into your credit report by telling you at whatever point another question is made.

13. You Will Be Told When another Record Is Made or Shut Credit checking may help you monitor your record of loan repayment by telling you at whatever point another record is opened or shut.

14. It assists you with watching out for your FICO rating. Credit checking administrations might help you in watching out for your FICO assessment by telling you at whatever point it goes through a change.

15. It makes it simpler to pursue wise monetary choices. Credit checking may make it more straightforward for you to settle on savvy monetary choices by telling you at whatever point there is an adjustment of your FICO rating. You'll be better prepared to make informed decisions about how to deal with your own cash because of this data.

The Most Effective Method To Monitor Your Credit

1. Check your credit report. One of the best strategies to watch out for your credit is to conduct continuous investigations into your credit report. One time per year, you are qualified to get a free duplicate of your credit report from every one of the three fundamental credit organisations, which are Equifax, Experian, and TransUnion. Assuming you have been turned down for credit, protection, or work because of data that was found in your credit report, you are likewise qualified to get a free duplicate of your credit report.

2. Keep up with Consistent Watchfulness over Your FICO Rating The three-digit figure that addresses your financial soundness is known as your FICO rating. Your FICO is not

entirely settled by the data remembered for your acknowledge reports, for example, your instalment history, the level of accessible credit that you use, and the various types of credit you have. Various visa guarantors and other monetary associations will readily furnish you with a free duplicate of your FICO rating upon demand.

3. Introduce Extortion Alarms: Introducing misrepresentation cautions is an incredible way to shield yourself from data fraud and check your FICO rating simultaneously. At the point when you put a misrepresentation caution on your credit report, the credit department will reach you right away in the event that somebody endeavours to enrol another record utilising your own data. You might put a misrepresentation caution on your credit report by calling the credit departments or doing so on the web.

4. Pursue Credit Checking Administrations: To watch out for your FICO rating, you ought to pursue credit-observing administrations. These administrations will tell you when there are any changes made shockingly report, remembering the kickoff of another record for your name. Free credit checking services might be gotten from different monetary organisations, including those that offer Mastercards.

5. Accounts from Your Bank and Mastercards Ought to Continuously Be Investigated It is fundamental to look at your bank and financial records consistently to guarantee that there have been no unlawful purchases. Assuming you see whatever appears to be off-putting, you ought to reach out to your bank or the organisation that gave you your charge card right away.

6. Check the movement on your visa. Many organisations that give Mastercards have online offices that empower you to monitor the action on your charge card. These devices might tell you, assuming there are any purchases that appear to be sketchy, or, on the other hand, in the event that your Mastercard is used in a spot that is uncommon to you.

7. Keep a Normal Observing Timetable for Your Speculation Records In the event that you have venture accounts, keeping a standard checking plan for those records is fundamental. You really want to ensure that your ventures are completed as expected and that there have been no unlawful exchanges.

8. Check the compensations on your Mastercard. Many organisations that give Visas offer rewards programmes that

empower cardholders to bring in cash or money back on purchases made with the card. It is fundamental to check your prize balance consistently if you have any desire to ensure you are taking advantage of the prize programme you are participating in.

9. Register for web-based banking. Doing your betting on the Web could help you stay on top of your funds. You can screen the equilibriums of your records, get cash across records, and set up alarms to be advised of any sketchy way of behaving.

10. Lay out programmed instalments. To keep your funds steady, one thing you ought to do is lay out programmed instalments for your bills. You have the choice of setting up your Visa instalments, contract instalments, and credit instalments for your vehicle to be paid accordingly.

11. Utilise a Planning Application: Planning applications can help you monitor your spending and stay on top of your monetary circumstances. There are a tonne of applications that let you make financial plans and monitor your investments in genuine energy.

12. Watch out for the loan fees on your Visas. The financing costs on charge cards can change contingent upon various variables, including your FICO assessment. It is fundamental to watch out for the loan costs related to your charge cards to guarantee that you are getting the most minimal rate conceivable.

13. Watch out for the constraints of your Mastercards. Your Visa limit is the maximum amount that can be charged to your card at

some random time. It is fundamental to monitor your Visa limit to ensure that you don't spend more than the distributed sum.

14. Monitor the awards on your charge card. Many Visa guarantors offer prize programmes that empower cardholders to bring in cash or money back on purchases made with their cards. It is crucial to check your prize balance on a regular basis to ensure you are capitalising on the prize programme you are taking chapter in.

15. Watch out for the expenses related to your visa. Many Mastercard guarantors survey expenses for explicit administrations, for example, moving an equilibrium or getting a loan. It is fundamental to monitor the expenses related to your charge card to guarantee that you are not paying more than needed.

<h2>Chapter 9</h2>

Key 8: Computerise Your Investment Funds

The accomplishment of monetary security is an essential goal for some individuals, and one of the best systems for arriving at this goal is to set up a programmed reserve fund plan. You can set aside cash without mulling over everything on the off chance that you robotize your investment funds, and this can be an extraordinary method for guaranteeing that you are reliably setting cash aside for your future.

The primary thing you really want to do while setting up a programmed reserve fund plan is to choose how much cash you need to take care of every month. This ought to be a total that you can pay without burning through every last dollar, yet it ought to likewise be sufficient to essentially affect your future funds. At the point when you have picked the sum, you may next lay out a common exchange that moves cash from your financial records to your bank account around the same time every month. This won't just make it more probable that you will get a good deal consistently; it will likewise make it simpler for you to oppose the longing to spend the cash, all things considered.

Computerising your reserve funds is helpful for various reasons, one of which is that it might help you keep up with your monetary goals. You will actually want to rapidly keep tabs on your development and guarantee that you are continually hitting your reserve fund objectives, assuming you set up a programmed move. This will make it undeniably more probable that you will arrive at your goals. On the off chance that you have a drawn-out monetary objective, such as putting something aside for retirement, this may be an exceptionally compelling technique for you to carry out.

In conclusion, to get the most out of accumulating funds, you ought to consider robotizing your recoveries. In the event that you get a good deal consistently, you will actually want to expand how much premium you get on the cash you have saved over the long haul. This might make it more straightforward for you to accomplish your monetary goals and influence your reserve funds to increase at an even faster rate.

Putting cash down for your future consistently may be testing, yet you can make it more straightforward on yourself by mechanising your investment funds. As well as helping you arrive at your money-related targets, it could make it more straightforward for you to exploit the advantages of self-multiplying dividends. You might ensure that you are continually setting aside cash and gaining ground towards your monetary targets, assuming you set up a robotized move from your financial records to your bank account every month. This move will transfer the cash from your financial records to your investment account.

Advantages Of Computerising Your Reserve Funds

1. Computerising your reserve funds simplifies it and makes it easier to save more assets, which prompts an expansion in the rate at which you set aside cash. You might raise your investment fund rate without investing any more mental energy into it by having cash saved for reserve funds deducted consistently from your compensation or financial balance.

2. Mechanising your reserve funds could help you abstain from making indiscreet purchases by reducing how much cash you spend on things you don't need to bother with. You will be less inclined to squander cash on pointless purchases on the off chance that you have consistently deducted cash from your compensation or financial balance to put towards your investment funds.

3. Computerising your investment funds permits you to achieve your objectives. All the more rapidly using your reserve funds naturally permits you to rapidly accomplish your monetary objectives. You may quickly develop your reserve funds and draw nearer to accomplishing your targets on the off chance that you orchestrate to have cash deducted from your compensation or ledger consistently for investment fund purposes.

4. Robotizing your investment funds permits you to abstain from overspending. Mcchanising your reserve funds permits you to abstain from overdoing it with your spending. At the point when you have cash consistently removed from your compensation or ledger, you are less inclined to make purchases that are more costly than they are within your means.

5. Computerising your reserve funds can assist you with remaining motivated. Doing your reserve funds in a robotized way can assist you with remaining spurred. The demonstration of having cash deducted consistently from your check or ledger can act as a helpful wake-up call to keep you on target with the monetary goals you've set for yourself.

6. Computerising your investment funds might assist you with staying away from late expenses. When you robotize your investment funds, you might observe that you can keep away from late charges. You can guarantee that your bills are paid on time and avoid causing late charges if you set up programmed reserve fund withdrawals from either your check or your financial balance.

7. Robotizing your reserve funds might assist you with building a secret stash. Doing so may assist you with building a Rainy Day account. Mechanising your reserve funds might help you do so. You may quickly develop your secret stash and be prepared for any unanticipated requirements, assuming you set it up so reserve funds are naturally deducted from your check or from the financial balance you keep the cash in.

8. Reserve Funds Programming Can Help You Accomplishing Your Retirement Goals: Investment fund programming might help you gather your drawn-out monetary targets, like retirement. You may quickly develop your retirement investment funds and prepare yourself for retirement, assuming you set them up to such an extent that your commitments are consequently deducted from either your check or your ledger.

9. Having your investment funds mechanised can assist you in putting something aside for big purchases. Having your investment funds done naturally can assist you with putting something aside for enormous purchases. You may quickly set aside sufficient cash for a critical buy and be in a monetary situation to pay for it, assuming you set up a computerised reserve fund plan that deducts cash from your compensation or from your financial balance.

10. Mechanising your reserve funds helps you stay focused. Computerising your investment funds might help you stay on track with your numerous money-related goals. You might ensure that you are continually setting aside cash and that you are on target to accomplish your financial goals by assigning a chapter of every check or ledger equilibrium to be moved into an investment account. By having

cash removed from your check or ledger consistently, you can ensure that you are continuously taking care of cash and being prepared for what's in store.

11. Mechanising your reserve funds can assist you with putting something aside for startling costs. Assuming you robotize your investment funds, you might observe that you are better prepared to put something aside for unexpected expenses. You may quickly gather an asset for dealing with unexpected expenses in the event that you organise to have cash saved for reserve funds deducted either straightforwardly from your compensation or from a ledger connected to your financial records.

12. Mechanising your reserve funds can help you put something aside for get-aways. Robotizing your reserve funds can help you set aside cash

for excursions. You can undoubtedly put something aside for an outing and have the cash open when you want it in the event that you have your reserve funds regularly deducted from your compensation or financial balance. This permits you to set aside cash in a helpful way.

13. Robotizing your investment funds can assist you with maintaining discipline. Having your reserve funds done naturally can assist you with keeping up with your discipline. You might keep yourself from falling victim to the enticement and assurance that you are saving money consistently by setting up a programmed withdrawal from your check or financial balance to go towards your reserve funds.

Instructions To Automate Your Reserve Funds

1. Lay out repeating computerised moves. One of the most straightforward ways of mechanising your investment funds is to lay out repeating, programmed moves from your financial records to your bank account consistently. You have the choice of booking the exchange to occur around the same time of the week or month, or you can plan a repetitive exchange to happen around the same time of the week or month.

2. Put aside the utilisation of direct installation. On the off chance that your work environment permits direct store, you have the choice of having a specific measure of cash from every check sent straightforwardly into your investment account consistently. This is a phenomenal strategy to set cash aside without putting any thought into it.

3. Utilise a Reserve Funds Application. There are various applications that might help you in mechanising your investment funds, and you ought to utilise one of these applications. Most of these applications empower you to gather together your purchases and send the distinction to your investment account, as well as set up repeating instalments in your investment account.

4. Lay out Programmed Instalments for Commitments On the off chance that you have charges that are expected consistently, for example, an instalment for an understudy loan or a vehicle instalment, you might lay out your financial records to consequently make instalments. You will not need to worry about whether you'll make sure to make the regularly scheduled instalment, assuming that you do it along these lines.

5. Design Your Venture Record to Make Programmed Commitments Assuming that you as of now have a speculation account, you might arrange your financial records to make programmed commitments to your venture account. This is an incredible technique for guaranteeing that you are consistently placing cash into ventures and creating your financial wellbeing.

6. Lay out programmed bank accounts. Monetary organisations furnish clients with the chance to lay out programmed bank accounts, which empower clients to have a foreordained measure of cash moved from their financial records to their investment account consistently. This is a phenomenal technique to set cash to the side without placing any thought into it.

7. Lay out Month-to-Month Standard Instalments on Your MasterCard Assuming you have a charge card, you can lay out month-to-month programmed instalments that are deducted from your financial records. Along these lines, you will not at any point be late with an instalment, and you won't miss a cutoff time for taking care of your obligation, by the same token.

8. Layout: Month-to-Month Investment Fund Objectives Numerous monetary foundations give clients the capacity to lay out month-to-month investment objectives and have their monetary organisation naturally move cash into their bank accounts consistently. This is a magnificent system to take care of cash for a specific reason, similar to an outing or another vehicle, for instance.

9. Utilise a planning application. There are various planning programmes that might help you mechanise your reserve funds, and you ought to utilise one of these applications. A lot of these applications give you the capacity to design out your funds, monitor your consumption, and even programme in customary stores to your bank account.

10. Utilise a Mastercard That Offers Money Back Assuming that you use a Visa that offers cash back, you might arrange to have the money back remunerations put into your bank account every month. This is a phenomenal strategy to set cash aside without putting any thought into it.

11. Lay out Programmed Reserve Fund Cautions Numerous monetary establishments give investment funds alarms that will send you an email or instant message when the equilibrium

in your investment account hits a specific limit. This is a superb technique for observing your financial circumstances and guaranteeing that you are on the correct path towards accomplishing your objectives.

12. Programme nth-to-month S Suggestions to Set Aside Cash You might programme the month-to-month's suggestions to set aside cash either on your telephone or on your PC. These updates will prompt you to move cash from your financial records to your bank account on the first of every month. This is a marvellous way to deal, guaranteeing that you are getting a good deal consistently.

13. Utilise a high-return investment account. Many banks currently offer high-return investment accounts, which provide clients with financing costs that are more noteworthy than those of standard bank accounts. This is

a phenomenal procedure for supporting the rate at which your assets collect.

14. Lay out a robotized reserve fund plan. A few monetary organisations reward clients with extra investment fund benefits in the event that they lay out a programmatic investment fund plan. This is a superb way to deal with getting some more pay consistently.

15. Utilise a Reserve Funds mini-computer. You can find various web-based investment fund number crunchers that will help you decide how much cash you want to put aside every month to meet your investment fund targets. You might use this as a supportive instrument to guarantee that you are not veering off from the arrangement.

Chapter 10

Key 9: Create Financial Stability.

The achievement of long-term monetary security is an objective that is essential to countless people, yet it is rarely accomplished. Expanding one's cash is a fundamental stage on the way to arriving at financial security, and achieving this goal ought to be vital for everybody. Expanding one's abundance is achieved by continuously gathering resources over a period of time. This might be finished in various ways. Putting away cash, setting up a reserve fund plan, and adhering to a spending plan are the three most incessant ways of hoarding riches.

One of the most fundamental exercises for collecting cash is effective financial planning. Contributing empowers you to take care of your cash to work for you and for it to increase throughout the span of time. Contributing might be achieved through a great many vehicles, including stocks, securities, shared assets, and, surprisingly, land. It is fundamental to comprehend the dangers that are associated with effective money management and to ensure that you are putting resources into something suitable for you if you have any desire to exploit the possible advantages of putting resources into a request to foster riches.

Putting cash down for sometime later is an extra crucial stage in the gathering of riches. The demonstration of setting cash aside for later use might be achieved in various ways, and setting aside cash offers you that chance. Currency market accounts, investment accounts, and store authentications are superb strategies to put cash down for what's to come. It is critical to remember that setting cash aside for a stormy day isn't equivalent to making a venture, and it is similarly fundamental to know about the qualifications between the two.

The production of a spending plan is an extra urgent move towards the method involved with hoarding wealth. Making a financial plan enables you to deal with your funds and guarantee that you are spending your cash in a dependable way. Making a spending plan might assist you with setting aside cash, and it can likewise assist you with putting resources into the fitting areas at the ideal opportunities. The production of a spending plan is an essential move towards the most common way of gathering cash and is suggested for all people.

The collection of cash is a basic chapter of the time spent arriving at a condition of monetary strength. Taking care of cash in the bank, taking care of cash in the financial exchange, and adhering to a spending plan are fundamental stages during the time spent hoarding riches, and they are objectives that everybody should pursue. The gathering of cash is an interaction that could require some investment; however, it is something that everybody should work for. Anybody can accumulate riches and achieve monetary solidity, assuming they utilise the fitting techniques and set forth the essential measure of energy.

Advantages Of Creating Financial Wellbeing

1. True serenity with regards to your monetary circumstances: Collecting cash gives you genuine serenity with regards to your monetary circumstances since it empowers you to have a security net to return to in case of an unexpected use or emergency. It likewise gives you the opportunity to settle on decisions about your life that, in any case, you probably won't have had the option to make. In the event that you hadn't had this opportunity, you probably wouldn't have had the option to pursue those decisions.

2. Reserve funds for Retirement: Amassing abundance enables you to put something aside

for retirement, which makes you ready to have an agreeable and agreeable way of life in your later years.

3. The Capacity to Make Ventures Collecting abundance gives you the valuable chance to make investments in resources like stocks, securities, and land, all of which can possibly create a reliable stream of pay.

4. Advantages to One's Monetary Position: Aggregating abundance might bring about ideal expense treatment, as specific ventures might fit the bill for deductions or credits.

5. Leaving an Inheritance: Gathering abundance offers you the chance to abandon something for your family and for people in the future.

6. Creating financial momentum enables you to settle on choices without considering the

effect those choices will have on your monetary circumstances.

7. Inner serenity. Collecting cash might create a feeling of smoothness, as it tells you that you have the monetary means to really focus on yourself and your friends and family.

8. Cash That Might Be Passed Down to People in the Future Collecting abundance can be a stage towards making generational riches, which empowers current abundance to be passed down to kids and grandkids.

9. An Expansion in Your Confidence Gathering cash gives you more impact over your own monetary fate, which might provide you with a more noteworthy feeling of satisfaction in yourself.

10. Monetary Autonomy: Amassing abundance empowers one to follow their expectations and desires without being obliged by worries over their capacity to monetarily support themselves.

11. Monetary Training Getting cash may give you the opportunity to look into individual accounting and speculation, which can furnish you with the data to pursue informed decisions about your monetary future.

12. Giving to a Good Cause and Issues You Care about Gathering abundance could offer chances to reward your local area with magnanimous commitments to associations and causes that mean a lot to you.

13. Wellbeing Nets: Gathering cash might give security nets looking like protection, speculations, and bank accounts, which can all

be utilised to aid the arrangement of help for one as well as one's family on account of an emergency.

14. Building cash might bring a liberating sensation from the pressure brought about by monetary worries, empowering you to focus on different components of your life during the time spent collecting riches.

15. Opportunity Collecting wealth gives you the freedom to pick chapters of your life that you, in any case, might not have had the option to decide because of an absence of choices.

Techniques For Creating Financial Stability

1. Put resources into the financial exchange. One of the most continuous and fruitful procedures to secure cash is to make investments in the securities exchange. You might enhance your possessions, increase your pay, and increase your true capacity for long-term gain, assuming you put resources into stocks.

2. Make an Interest in Land One of the most mind-blowing ways of accumulating wealth is to make an interest in land. Putting resources into land might offer you a dependable source of revenue, notwithstanding the likelihood that the worth of your property will increase over the long haul.

3. Lay out your own organisation. Laying out your own organisation is an incredible method

for aggregating wealth. Make an organisation that can furnish you with a salary and can possibly increase your self-esteem over time by giving you gifts and giving you something to do.

4. Set Cash Aside and Contribute It: Taking care of cash and giving it something to do is quite possibly one of the main things you can do to foster your riches. It is basic to set aside a portion of your profit and set those reserve funds to work as interests in a different arrangement of resources.

5. Remain within your means. One of the best techniques for gathering cash is to keep a way of life that doesn't surpass one's monetary assets. To store up cash throughout some undefined time frame, it is vital to keep one's spending at a level that is lower than one's pay and to contribute to the distinction.

6. Dispense with All Obligations: Disposing of every one of one's obligations is perhaps the most fundamental stage during the time spent aggregating abundance. It is essential to take care of exorbitant premium obligations as quickly as possible to let loose more cash for money management and saving. This might be achieved by taking care of obligations as quickly as possible.

7. Put your reserve funds on autopilot. Putting your reserve funds on autopilot is an incredible system to ensure that you are saving and contributing consistently. You can consistently move cash from your financial records to your investment account or venture account by setting up repeating mechanised moves.

8. Utilise Records That Can Decrease Your Taxation Rate: Putting cash in vehicles that

give good assessment treatment might be a viable procedure for gathering abundance. These records, for example, 401(k)s, IRAs, and HSAs, give you the potential to set aside and put cash in a way that delays or kills the effect of making good on charges.

9. Expand your resources. If you have any desire to develop abundance, quite possibly one of the main strategies you can use is to spread your cash around in various kinds of speculations. If you have any desire to enhance your benefits while limiting your openness to risk, it is fundamental to differentiate your ventures among an extensive variety of resource types.

10. Capitalise on Compounding: Compounding is perhaps the most impressive power in the realm of effective money management, and it very well might be a phenomenal strategy to

foster abundance throughout an extensive stretch of time. At the point when you reinvest the benefits you make from your ventures, an interaction known as intensifying happens, which makes those speculations extend at a faster speed.

11. Make speculations with a drawn-out point of view. Making ventures with an expansive viewpoint is one of the best strategies for gathering cash. It is vital to draw out the force of compounding and decrease the gamble of momentary market unpredictability. Contributing for the long haul likewise assists you with exploiting the force of compounding.

12. Utilise minimising risk. Taking advantage of mitigating risk is a fabulous system to create financial wellbeing over time. Speculation of a foreordained amount of cash at ordinary

stretches is the foundation of this method, which is planned to moderate the effect of the unpredictability intrinsic in securities exchange money management.

13. Limit your expenses. Bill and Foster Abundance After some time, by exploiting the Misfortune Gathering Assessment: Misfortune collection is a staggering procedure to diminish how much cash you owe in charges and to create financial momentum over the long run. The reason for this strategy is to lessen the effect of paying cxpenses on capital increases by selling resources that have seen a fall in value.

14. Capitalise on Your Boss' Matching Advantages A magnificent method for storing up abundance is to exploit your manager's matching advantages. Most managers will, up to a foreordained cutoff, contribute an

equivalent amount to a retirement account for the representative's benefit, for example, a 401(k) or comparative arrangement.

15. Make an interest in yourself. Making an interest in yourself is quite possibly one of the most fundamental things you can do to create your financial momentum. It is fundamental to make interests in your schooling, abilities, and information to raise your procuring potential and create financial stability throughout the span of your functioning life.

Chapter 11

Key 10: Teach Yourself.

Many individuals have the goal of achieving monetary security, yet not very many know about the means necessary to achieve it. Advancing however much you can about how to keep up with your monetary stability is the main move towards accomplishing this goal. Assuming you approach the fitting data and assets, you will actually want to go with the instructed decisions that will carry you closer to achieving financial security.

Understanding your ongoing monetary circumstances is the most important phase in teaching yourself the best way to keep up with your monetary soundness over the long haul. This includes having a strong handle on your monetary circumstances regarding your pay, costs, obligations, and investment funds. It is fundamental for your objective of achieving monetary solidity to know where your cash is going and the amount you have available to work with. After you have acquired a superior comprehension of your ongoing monetary circumstances, you can then start to make changes to further develop them.

The next thing you really want to do is make a spending plan. An arrangement that determines how your cash will be spent is referred to as a spending plan. Your pay, your costs, your obligations, and your reserve funds ought to be included in every way. You'll have the option to watch your spending and decide if you're living within your means in the event that you make and adhere to a financial plan.

You must start a reserve fund plan when you have a functioning spending plan set up. Having a strong monetary establishment requires a lot of reserve funds. It can make it more straightforward for you to develop a secret stash, which is cash that can be used to take care of unexpected expenses. Also, it can help you set aside cash for your retirement and other long-term targets.

To wrap things up, maintaining an elevated degree of monetary literacy is fundamental. Keeping yourself informed can assist you with pursuing better choices and keep you on track to accomplish the monetary objectives you have set for yourself. You can achieve this objective by perusing monetary magazines, going to courses on monetary points, or signing up for classes regarding the matter.

The most vital move towards achieving monetary solidity is to teach oneself the point. You will actually want to settle on taught choices that will help you achieve monetary solidity in the event that you first gain a comprehension of your ongoing monetary circumstances, make a spending plan, then set aside cash, and lastly, keep yourself informed. Taking advantage of your cash and achieving monetary security are the two objectives that are within your scope, assuming you approach them with the appropriate data and assets.

Advantages Of Monetary Instruction

1. Increased monetary proficiency People who have gotten sufficient monetary instruction have a superior comprehension of the essentials of cash management, including planning and money management. This can possibly bring about expanded monetary proficiency. This can help individuals make more educated decisions about their monetary circumstances, which can eventually prompt expanded monetary steadiness.

2. An expansion in how much cash is saved Individuals who have gotten monetary schooling are bound to comprehend the meaning of setting aside cash and the most effective strategies for doing so. Individuals who do this might have the option to set aside more cash and gather savings that they can

use for retirement or other long-term objectives.

3. Better Monetary Arrangement People who have gotten sufficient monetary schooling are better prepared to understand the basics of monetary preparation and how to build a spending plan. People can involve this for their own potential benefit, as far as making arrangements for the future and guaranteeing they are on target to accomplish their money-related goals.

4. Diminished Commitment to Take Care of Obligations Getting schooled in individual accounting can help people understand the essentials of their obligations to the board and how to diminish how much cash they owe. Individuals who do this can take care of their obligations all the more rapidly and wind up setting aside cash in general over the long haul.

5. A positive FICO rating People can profit from understanding the essentials of credit and how to further develop their FICO ratings with the help of monetary schooling. This makes it feasible for individuals to get lower loan costs on credits and other monetary items.

6. Expanded Speculation Information People can profit from expanded venture information by better comprehending the basics of effective money management and how to make insightful monetary choices. The collection of riches and the achievement of one's monetary goals can both be worked with.

7. Better Anticipating Retirement With the help of monetary schooling, people can acquire a superior comprehension of the basics of

retirement planning and how to make an arrangement for themselves. It is workable for this to help people save adequate assets for retirement and guarantee an agreeable way of life during their brilliant years.

8. Further developed monetary security People can acquire a superior comprehension of the basics of monetary security and how to shield their resources with the assistance of monetary instruction. This might assist with people having high expectations about their monetary circumstances while likewise guaranteeing that their cash is secured.

9. Better Capacity to Make Keen Choices In regards to cash monetary schooling might help individuals understand the essentials of monetary navigation and show them how to make smart decisions with regard to their cash. This might help individuals further develop their decisions about their cash and

accomplish the monetary targets they set for themselves.

10. Diminished Probability of Being a Survivor of Monetary Extortion Getting sufficient monetary education might help individuals fathom the basics of monetary misrepresentation and figure out how to defend themselves from it. This might help individuals by keeping them from being survivors of monetary misrepresentation and safeguarding the cash they have endeavoured to acquire.

11. Expanded Monetary Certainty: People might have a superior comprehension of the basics of cash management and how to pursue sound monetary decisions with the help of monetary training. Individuals who do this could work on their feeling of safety about

their monetary circumstances and guarantee that their cash is buckling down for them.

12. Further developed monetary propensities

People can acquire a superior comprehension of the essentials of monetary propensities and how to foster great cash the executive's propensities with the help of monetary training. This can help people foster a spending plan and stay unfaltering to it, which eventually prompts them to work on their monetary wellbeing.

13. An Expansion in Monetary Open Doors

People can be helped with understanding the basics of monetary open doors and how to take advantage of them through monetary schooling. People can profit from this by finding better approaches to bringing in cash and creating their financial wellbeing.

14. Expanded Monetary Steadiness People who have gotten monetary schooling might have a superior comprehension of the basics of monetary solidity as well as the means important to accomplish it. This can help people have a real sense of reassurance about their monetary circumstances while likewise guaranteeing that their cash is really buckling down for them.

15. More noteworthy monetary freedom People can acquire a superior comprehension of the basics of monetary freedom and how to achieve it with the help of monetary training. Individuals who do this can build their possibilities by carrying on with the existence of monetary freedom and guaranteeing that their cash is buckling down for them.

Assets For Monetary Instruction

1. Monetary Proficiency Instruction Projects: These are programmes that are meant to help individuals handle the basics of monetary education, for example, making a spending plan, setting aside cash, putting away cash, and various other points. These projects are often made accessible by instructive foundations, local gatherings, and monetary establishments.

2. Sites That Give Monetary Schooling There are a wide variety of sites that are dedicated to offering monetary training. These sites frequently provide various instructive apparatuses, including articles, recordings, and different media, to help customers increase their insight into individual accounting.

3. Seminars on monetary training A wide assortment of foundations and schools offer classes on individual budgets. People might get a superior handle on how to deal with their funds with the help of these courses, which can give a total survey of various monetary issues.

4. Applications for Monetary Training There is a scope of applications accessible that might help shoppers acquire a more profound comprehension of their particular monetary circumstances. These applications frequently provide customers with devices for planning, venture direction, and different assets that help people pursue better monetary decisions.

5. Books on Monetary Schooling There is a wide determination to make writing accessible, which might help individuals extend their insight into their individual budget. These

distributions frequently give top-to-bottom direction on a large number of subjects, including monetary preparation, financial exchange examinations, and significantly more.

6. Courses on Monetary Schooling: There are various gatherings that give studios on an individual budget. People might get a superior handle on how to deal with their funds with the help of these classes, which can give a total survey of different issues connected with funds.

7. Recordings for Monetary Schooling People hoping to extend their insight into individual accounting could profit from watching one of the numerous recordings that are presently available. These movies frequently give top-to-bottom data on a great many subjects,

including monetary preparation, venture methodologies, and other related matters.

8. Monetary Training Digital recordings: People who are keen on advancing more about individual accounting could profit from paying attention to one of the many webcasts that are presently accessible on the point. These web recordings frequently give top-to-bottom data on a great many subjects, including monetary preparation, speculation procedures, and other related matters.

9. Sites for monetary training: There is a wide choice of web journals on the web that individuals might peruse to more deeply study dealing with their own funds. These web journals frequently give top-to-bottom data on a large number of subjects, including monetary preparation, venture procedures, and other related matters.

10. Bulletins for Monetary Instruction People hoping to grow their insight into individual budgets could profit from perusing one of the numerous pamphlets that are currently accessible. These distributions frequently give top-to-bottom inclusion of a large number of issues, including monetary preparation, speculation techniques, and other related matters.

11. Monetary Schooling Classes Various associations offer courses on the subject of individual budgets. People might profit from these courses by acquiring a superior handle on how to deal with their funds and a comprehensive outline of various issues connected with funds.

12. Worksheets for Monetary Training There are a wide variety of worksheets accessible that

individuals might use to dive more deeply into dealing with their own funds. These worksheets frequently contain top-to-bottom data on a range of subjects, including planning, money management, and various different themes.

13. Games for monetary training: There are a variety of games that are open to individuals that might help them become familiar with individual accounting. The player might get top-to-bottom information on a large number of subjects by playing these games, including money, ventures, and some more.

14. Recordings for Monetary Schooling: There are a wide variety of recordings that are presently open that might help individuals gain insight into individual accounting. These movies frequently give inside-and-out data on a great many subjects, including monetary

preparation, venture methodologies, and other related matters.

15. Sites Committed to Monetary Schooling: There are various sites on the web that are dedicated to showing individuals their funds. These sites frequently provide various instructional apparatuses, including articles, recordings, and different media, to help shoppers increase their insight into their individual budgets.

Chapter 12

Last Considerations On Monetary Security

Solidarity in one's monetary circumstances is a fundamental thought that has repercussions for individuals and organisations as well as for entire countries. A precarious thought relies upon a wide assortment of things, including the extension of the economy, the pace of expansion, and the financing cost. Dependability in the monetary area is basic to the extension and support of a sound economy since it empowers both confidential families and business undertakings to devise strategies for the future and participate in capital uses.

For legislatures to achieve monetary security, it is essential for them to take measures to ensure that their economies are strong and expanding. This includes setting in motion strategies that empower financial extension, for example, bringing down charge rates and collecting how much cash the public authority spends. It likewise involves taking measures to cut down on expansion and keep loan fees at generally low levels. It is likewise the obligation of legislatures to safeguard the dependability of their money-related frameworks and the legitimate guidelines of the financial business.

People and companies both have a role to play during the time spent making monetary security, notwithstanding the strategies that are sanctioned by the public authority. Great monetary administration ought to be polished by people, including making a financial plan and setting aside cash for what's in store. Furthermore, organisations need to confirm that they have a solid monetary standing and that they are effectively attempting to reduce the dangers they face.

As a rule, the possibility of monetary soundness is huge since it affects individuals' lives as well as the existence of endeavours and entire countries. Great monetary administration is something that should not exclusively be polished by individuals and organisations but also by legislatures to ensure that their economies stay vigorous and keep on extending. Assuming we go to these lengths, we can guarantee that both of our economies will keep on being strong and that our monetary frameworks will keep on being hearty.

Conclusion

A hearty economy should have a solid monetary framework, first and foremost. It is urgent for customers, organisations, and state-run administrations to approach monetary administrations that are reliable and modest. Steadiness in the economy assists with ensuring that individuals, enterprises, and legislatures approach the assets they need to satisfy their monetary responsibilities and put resources into the eventual fate of their nation or area. Security in the monetary area likewise adds to the economy's protection against monetary shocks and to a decrease in the probability of monetary emergencies happening.

A blend of major areas of strength—strategies, savvy guidelines, and productive management of monetary foundations—is expected to achieve the objective of achieving monetary steadiness. The execution of compelling financial strategies might add to the economy's expansion in a manner that isn't just manageable but also assists with keeping expansion within acceptable limits. Powerful oversight assists with distinguishing and moderating any potential dangers, while judicious guidelines add to the confirmation that monetary establishments are doing their business in a solid and dependable manner.

One essentially can't stress the meaning of having stable funds. It is vital for customers, organisations, and legislatures to approach monetary administrations that are trustworthy and economical. Security in the economy assists with ensuring that individuals, enterprises, and legislatures approach the assets they need to satisfy their monetary responsibilities and put resources into the eventual fate of their nation or locale. Steadiness in the monetary area likewise adds to the economy's guard against monetary shocks and to a decrease in the probability of monetary emergencies happening. Because of these elements, it is fundamental for individuals, states, and monetary establishments to team up to propel the reason for monetary solidity.